Event Planning Tips

The Straight Scoop on How to Run a Successful Event

By
Natalie Johnson

Table of Contents

Introduction

I want to thank you and congratulate you for downloading the book, "Event Planning Tips: The Straight Scoop on How to Run a Successful Event"

Events management has been around for a while now, but it is only recently that the said industry became an important part of many economies. That isn't surprising though, since big events generate revenue and boost tourism. Take travel expos for instance, many are held every year to garner global attention. The World Olympics is another excellent example – it's held every four years and it never fails in boosting the host country's economy.

Given the number of visitors that these events attract, it is no wonder why they're seen as major activities in the tourism industry. This book aims to inform the readers of the perks of managing an event successfully. It also shows the importance of proper planning, marketing strategies, before-and-after organization, and developing the right skills to create memorable and magical events.

I hope that as you read on, you'd learn more about the events industry and how you could successfully be a part of it. Again, thank you for downloading this book! I hope you enjoy learning from it!

Chapter 1

What is an Event and What is Event Management?

The idea of conducting or hosting events came way before the beginning of modern civilization, when leaders of tribes or armies would gather to carry out peace talks and negotiations. Massive ceremonies (particularly those fueled by faith) were also held during the ancient times.

Today, events serve as social opportunities for people to strengthen their community, as well as spread awareness for causes that makes the community a better place. Events also get people together, letting them communicate and share their different cultures. Politically, gatherings signify power and popularity, they give people the chance to be heard by the government, resolve civic issues, celebrate national holidays, and discuss matters of public interest.

The events management industry contributes to the society's economic success, as it opens employment and investment opportunities. Sometimes, it indirectly strengthens a community's tourism potential.

The number of participants could be used to classify events. Small events are composed of up to 30 participants, medium-sized events are participated by up to 100 individuals, large events are attended by up to 300 participants, and mega events involve thousands of people going to one single destination. Those classifications could be further subdivided, according to the type (or nature) of the event.

- Personal Events

This includes life moments such as birthdays, anniversaries, baptisms, weddings, and other special personal events. The celebrant is generally the one who arranges personal events (there's usually no need for planners or coordinators to be involved).

- Educational/Career Events

These events are known to either impart knowledge to its attendees or provide career opportunities for them. Some examples of these events include job fairs, career advancement seminars, familiarization tours, field trips, conferences, and conventions.

- Sports Events

These are events where the main attractions are sports matches – the Winter Olympics, World Olympics, Basketball championship games, Wimbledon, and other happenings that involve sporting activities all fall under this category.

- Entertainment Events

Probably the most well known event type, entertainment events are done to provide a more relaxed environment that entertains the attendees. Concerts, stage plays, stand-up comedies, and pageants are some good examples of these events.

- Political Events

Political events show or solicit support from people regarding a particular issue or cause. Examples of this type of event are rallies, public demonstrations, and campaigns.

- Corporate Events (MICE)

Corporate events are held mainly to inform the market of a corporation's existing products and services, to launch or promote a new product, or to strengthen public relations.

Meetings, incentive travels, conferences and expositions (MICE), product launches, trade shows and product exhibits are just some of the most commonly held corporate events.

- Religious/Cultural Events

This includes festivals, religious ceremonies, cultural fairs, heritage museum tours, and cultural shows.
All of those highlight the unique qualities of different cultures and religions.

This kind of event aims to promote a locality's culture, which in turn adds appeal to the place as a tourist destination.

- Non-profit/Cause-related Events

As the name suggests, this type of event's main purpose is to raise funds, spread awareness, and support a certain cause. Here are several events that fall under this subcategory – fund-raising galas, charity auctions, and volunteer drives.

Because of the momentum that the events industry has been gaining lately, event management a key factor in developing and creating events that are worth repeating every year.

Event management may be called by different names, but it is always beyond just knowing what you want to do and how you want your next event to look like. It involves the careful evaluation of the market (especially when it comes to demographics). Carrying out negotiations, doing some planning work, and mingling are also part of event management endeavors.

Planning your own event (or doing it for someone else) requires skills that would get you through all the haggling and the endless need to check every little detail.

Chapter 2

An Ideal Event Manager

It takes a lot of courage, patience, creativity, and wit to be an event manager or an event planner. Successful events require good food, lights, hosts, an organized program, and great entertainment. All these elements are the prime concerns of the event manager, aside from handling the stress that stems from meeting deadlines, making ends meet, and fitting everything into a tight schedule.

Successful event managers and planners have the following qualities that help them come up with gatherings that everyone would definitely remember:

1. Creativity and Flexibility
   If you want to organize an event like no other, prepare to rack your brains for ideas to make the event wonderfully unique. You may need (or want) different things to be in your event, so this means that an event planner must be able to conceptualize and put into reality all the elements in a creative manner.

In case things are not going according to plan, an event manager should be able to adapt (sometimes this even involves the need to come up with an entirely new plan).

2. Keen eye for details
   Not all people have the sharpest eye for details. However, minute details are still part of the event, so an event planner should always pay attention to such seemingly unimportant things.

3. Organizing skills
   The very best event managers all have ability to manage people, be on schedule, and juggle between client and supplier meetings.

   Food tastings, visual inspections, bargain hunting, and even menu selection are also among the many must-dos that an efficient event planner successfully completes.

4. Communication and negotiating skills
   Planning events will require you to talk to many people of different personalities – from entertainers to caterers, and from sound system providers to participants. It is important for a planner to know what to say and how to talk to people in an engaging and courteous manner.

This includes the ability to negotiate and persuade suppliers or service providers for more affordable prices or better deals. It is also important for an event specialist to know how to connect with people and build lasting relationships with both clients and suppliers. Having the ability to understand people, for the sake of working out client issues, is also vital.

5. Leadership skills
   Ordering people around just doesn't work in this kind of business because it creates a heavy atmosphere for everyone involved. What an event needs is a leader who could manage and motivate the team without snapping in the middle of all the things that are happening. This shows just how important it is to work hand-in-hand with the team and resolve problems together.

6. Ability to stay focused and calm
   No event progresses 100% smoothly. At one point, something will go wrong. An event planner should be able to maintain focus and remain calm even when things are going out of hand. This is to ensure that solving problems or looking for possible workarounds stay possible. An event manager should know that panicking never creates solutions.

7. Ability to Multitask

Event planning requires a lot of things to be done all at the same time. So, as a planner, it is your job to do everything all at once.

An event planer should know how to juggle tasks and perform activities that are not of the same nature. Still, remember that multitasking is not just about getting things done. It is a skill of getting multiple things done without making all sorts of mistakes.

Chapter 3

Planning for Your Event

For an event to be a complete success, planning is a necessary first step. Planning does not only let you prepare for possible problems, it gives you an idea of how your event should look like and what you need to get there.

Step 1: Know your goals and objectives
Knowing what you're doing the event for will make it easier for you to make a plan. Also, as you are thinking of what you want to achieve, you shouldn't forget that your plans and concepts must fit the needs of your client. Here are some sample goals and objectives:

- To create an event that will help raise funds for cancer awareness
- Organize a Paris-themed debutante ball for a friend's daughter

Simply put, know what kind of event you want to do – think about the theme, your target participants, the number of people you could allow, the event date, and your brand and tagline (for businesses-oriented happenings).

Step 2: Create an initial plan

Your initial plan should include your timeline or Gantt chart – a list of your prospective suppliers, tentative venue, list of topics and themes (for seminars, conferences, and conventions), sources of funds, preparation of permits, and other requirements. In addition, list down all things that you will possibly need for your event and how are you going to get them. When creating your tentative or initial list, take note of the following:

- You need at least four to six months to plan and organize your event. Planning events in a shorter period may not allow you to address other concerns and wouldn't give you the chance to look for alternatives.

- Be aware of permit requirements, school breaks, and religious holidays. It is best not to do an event during school breaks if your target participants are students, as they are expected to be out of their homes on those times for vacation.

- Know the availability of your key participants. Know what time would they be available, what date, and how long they'd be able to stay. You should inform your speakers, audiences, and VIP guests ahead of time so they could check their schedules and avoid time conflicts.

Step 3: Organize your team

You will need people to help you out, and that's not an optional element. Your work force (or in other words, your team) should be composed of people who are willing to work with you through thick and thin. Your team includes your master of ceremony, speakers, entertainers, caterers (or venue crew), volunteers, invitation publishers, designers, and choreographer. Of course, the composition of your team still depends on what kind of event you are going to organize.

Step 4: Establish your budget

After you have identified your needs, create a budget plan. A budget is a list of your probable income and expenditures. It provides an organized breakdown of how much you have, how much you should spend, and how much you'd have left. Creating a budget plan for an event will give you an idea of how much money you'd need and the amount of cash you'd have to raise.

It gives you an estimate of your financial status and gives you a clear picture of your financial goal.

Computer programs (such as electronic spreadsheets and budget applications) in tablets and mobile phones are available if you don't know how to start your plan.

The main thing is to list down everything you would need, allotting a specific amount for each. You will also need to list down your possible financial sources, and then add details on how much each would be willing to give you.

Step 5: Finalize your initial plan
Now that you have an idea of the things you would require and everything that those entail, you may now finalize your initial plan – or simply put, complete your master plan. You master plan will serve as your guide regarding the requirements for your event. Your master plan should include your final plans for (but not limited to):

- Program, activities, entertainment, venue
- Permit, insurance, and supplier contracts
- Participant registration process and fees, invitation, seating plans
- Publicity and promotional plan, sponsorship and/or solicitations
- Post-event evaluation plan

- Timeline

Step 6: Go through your plan and reevaluate
Once you're done with all your master plan, go through it one more time and be its first critic. Is it foolproof? Is it attainable? Do you have enough time to execute your plan?

Do you have enough money? You should ask questions about your plan and reevaluate it based on what you have found out. If you believe that some things should still be developed, or if you think some elements are still in need of polishing, you may want to consider developing a new plan (or at least a backup plan). Remember to come up with an alternative just in case your original plan doesn't work out. It's better to have something to replace things than having nothing and simply trying to make do in the end.

Chapter 4

Marketing Your Event

Especially true for commercial events, marketing comes even before the planning is all done. It is a common misconception that marketing is simply presenting a product or a service in an interesting way. That is not entirely true. Advertising is just one aspect of marketing, and marketing a service-oriented product (such as an event) will need careful considerations.

1. Packaging
   Question is, how would you create a packaging for an event? Of course, we're not talking about literally putting your event in a box. We are talking about how your clients, or potential audience in that matter, will perceive your event. Start with things that suit your theme, such as a pink zebra-inspired invitation for a girl's 18th birthday party or a more formal invite for a wedding ceremony. The important thing here is that you encourage your clients to participate by showing them what it would be like.

   Take time to plan your packaging.

If hotels have front offices to take care of the first impression, what you have is your idea and creativity. Make sure that all your communication letters, tickets, and VIP passes speak for the quality of your event.

2. Communications

You have so many channels of communication to choose from, but the best ones will always be those that match the preferences of your target audience. For example, if your aim is to entice women who are fond of reading the lifestyle section of the local paper, it might be wise to have your invitation published there (a half-page print will do). That way, you are sure that at one point, they'll see it. Sending an e-mail, using social media, going for snail mail, and showing interactive TV ads are some other excellent ways of "communicating" with your audience.

All these communication channels could be considered the best, depending on which aspect of communication are you looking at. For events though, the most effective is still "word of mouth."

Since your clients have no means of seeing the actual event that you're preparing before it's done, it is always best to boost your advertisements with positive and trusted endorsements from various people. You could talk to your former clients to get some referrals.

You could also encourage them to support your upcoming event by asking them to be a sponsor or an attendee.

3. An event before the event
   You can create a before-the-event gathering where participants could win special merchandise, or tempt them with free passes to the event proper. Aside from doing those things, get ideas on how you could improve your event by asking questions.

   A before-the-event happening is not exactly held to encourage attendance, but to stir curiosity. This will indirectly influence people's minds in coming to see what you have to offer.

4. Publicity or public relations
   Lastly, if you can't ask thousands to support you, ask someone to help you complete all the PR-related must-dos.

Here's a fact that might prove to be useful - people support those who back charities. If you're planning on creating a charity event, get help from someone who's an active supporter of your chosen cause. Particularly, ask that person to publicize your event or, in other words, encourage attendance.

Chapter 5

Pre-event Preparations

Most event planners and coordinators will agree when we say that the pre-event is always the most crucial part of the event itself. That is because you have to do everything before the event, and make sure that everything's in place and perfectly fine. Here are the things you need to do before the event:

Venue

The first step in preparing your event's venue is to go there for an ocular inspection. This step will allow you to confirm the capacity of your venue, and you'd also get an idea of what it actually looks like (thus helping you come up with a good floor plan). This should be done at least two months before the event, to give allowance to possible changes in venue (or to have enough time to alter your decoration plans).

It is important to point out that outdoor events are good options. Those events help you cut on expensive decorations, and they also let you work with nature to create a more natural and relaxed ambiance.

Outdoor events also give you more alternatives, as you are not confined to having your party inside your home or in a hall.

Also, check the size of the area that you could actually use. Of course, bigger events require bigger spaces. The question though, is this – what setup are you going for anyway? If you're arranging a seminar, a press conference, or something of the sort and you are not going to offer food and drinks, then a theater setup will be just fine. A stage, a podium, and a long table will be placed in front, while individual chairs will face the stage.

A classroom setup is great for workshops and other events that require participants to do something aside from listening (such as use a computer system or take notes during discussions). As for personal events (such as weddings, birthdays, and anniversaries), the buffet setup is a common choice.

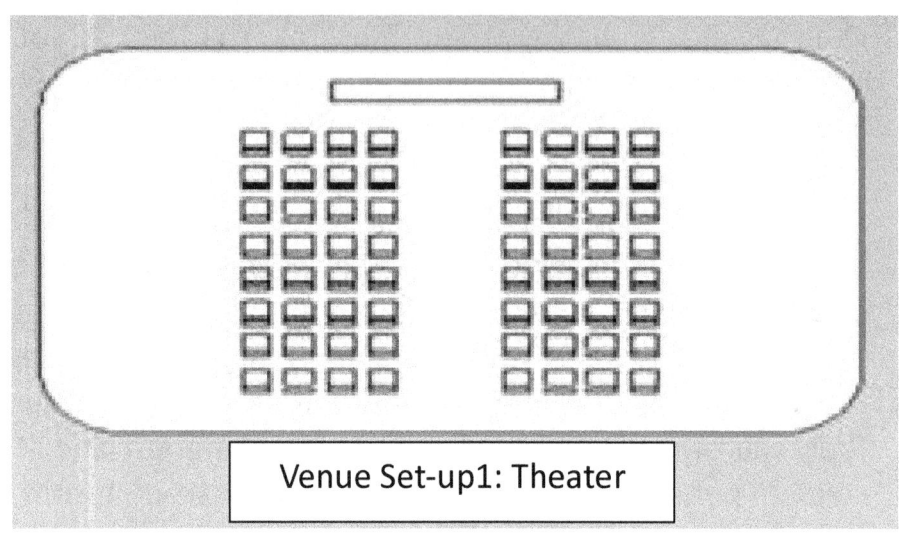

Venue Set-up1: Theater

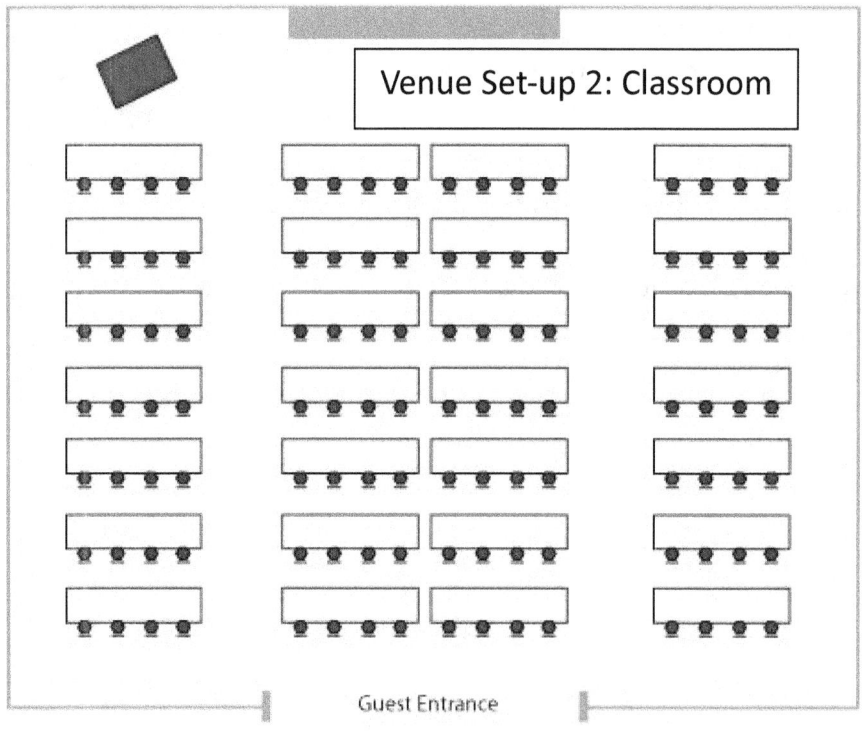

Venue Set-up 2: Classroom

Guest Entrance

21

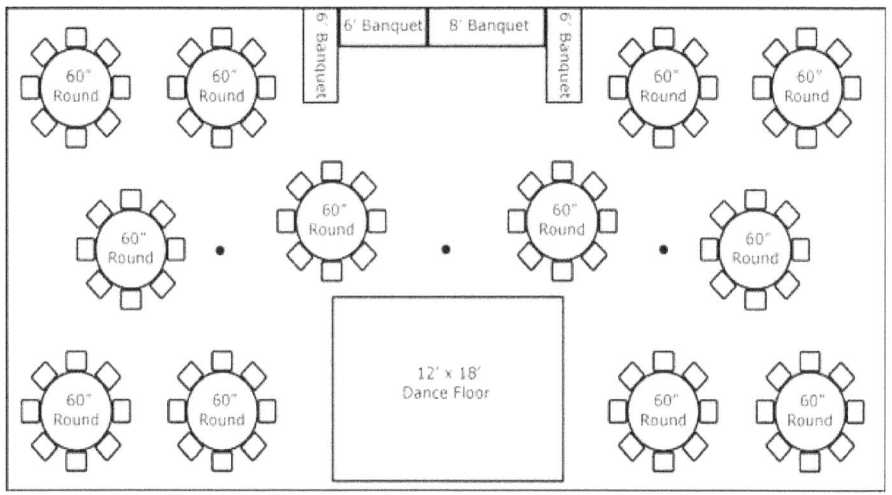

Venue Set-up 3: Buffet

No matter which setup you'd choose for the event, it should be appropriate for the occasion and the activities that are going to be done during the program. The size should also be enough to give attendees ample amount of leg room or sufficient space to move around and mingle.

Foods and drinks
Usually, caterers will provide you with a good selection of menus (with their corresponding costs). Minding your budget, how much food could you afford? Usually, food and beverages are the biggest items in a planner's budget list, so it is best to go for the option that offers the best value.

There are three basic ways to negotiate when it comes to food and drinks:

- Ask caterers for copies of their menu lists, and choose from their available packages
- Let the catering company know how much your budget is, and simply ask it to come up with a customized menu
- Tell the catering business what you want (by coming up with a menu of your own), and try to get an accurate estimate

Know what comes with the price. While some caterers will provide service crews and set-up teams, some don't.

Also, check whether the utensils and the equipment you need (such as tables, chairs, and cover cloths) would all be provided. Some caterers will only add those options if you're willing to spend an extra. It's fairly common for caterers to merely focus on your food and beverage needs.

If you and your team know people who could volunteer to help you out, it would be cheaper to ask these volunteers to act as your service crew and set-up crews.

However, if you have the budget anyway, opting for caterers who could provide you with everything you need would save you a lot of time.

It is always best to have a food-tasting meeting with your caterer before you settle for a menu. This will allow you to know if the food would go well with the event's theme. The idea is for you to know what your food would be like. You should carefully choose which items should stay and which ones need to be omitted. Some caterers who participate in fairs offer a free taste of their offerings, and even provide discounted packages if you'd book them during the event. If you could attend fairs like these, it would give you a better idea on which caterer really is the best.

Decorations
As mentioned before, outdoor events are always cheaper when it comes to decorations, as outdoor locations already have a distinct appeal and all you have to do is enhance them. Unfortunately, it would cost you a little more in transporting both your equipment and your attendees, especially if the place is remote and no public transportation is available (in case not everyone in your invited list has a car or no one's familiar with the location).

On a positive note, gone are the days when your only option in decorating is using expensive flowers that don't stay fresh for long.

As people became more creative and resourceful, cheaper things now have a space even in expensive events. For example, instead of the usual flower arrangements for centerpieces, people now use glasses or bowls with flower petals and floating candles.

Balloons have also replaced some functions for entrance arches, and lights could now be used in place of firework displays.

Still, the best decoration ideas are the ones that reflect your theme and set the right mood for your event. If it's a formal event, using balloons and tarpaulins may not be a good idea – unlike if they're used in more casual events, like feeding-programs or office farewell parties. You may also want to make use of colored glassware or long pieces of cloth to enhance your venue's visuals.

There are specialty shops that you can go to for special kinds of décor – the ones that that you could throw away after use, but are sturdy enough to be utilized in the next event. Bargain shops and department stores are also good go-to places for needs like these.

On the other hand, if you're on a tight budget, you could always search your own garage (or attic) for something useful.

Invitations and Souvenirs

Your invitations are supposed to be distributed at least three weeks before the actual event to give your guests time to check their schedules and respond to your RSVP. Nowadays, anyone with a computer can create a nice invitation card, as well as RSVP and Thank You cards. If you think you can't do this on your own and you don't have enough computer knowledge, searching for a publisher will be a wise choice.

Some invitation makers offer different layouts for different occasion (such as boarding passes, passports, admit-one tickets, and other more traditional cards). Just remember to put all the important information on your invites (such as reception venue, date and time of event, dress code and color motif, and the type of occasion). For weddings, the entourage list is usually enclosed in an envelope, together with the actual invitation.

As for the souvenirs, you could always have them done by experts in souvenir making, or you could make them yourself.

Different websites and video-sharing communities are available online, and they show you how to do souvenirs DIY-style with the help of craft stores and trinket shops nearby. Make your souvenir something the attendees will be able to use in the future.

Toiletry baskets, stationery sets, mini bottles of wine, or little key chains are now used in place of the traditional little figurines.

Some more informal events have photo booths that print pictures instantaneously. The pictures come designed with the event's theme, and are stamped with the date and place where the event took place.

RSVP and Seat Plan

As much as possible, you should have the RSVP slips returned to you at least two weeks before the event, so that you will have more time to alter your orders for food and re-plan your venue setup if necessary. You will also need to do that to monitor the count of your actual attendees, and to finalize the list of your invited guests (for private parties). Also, the RSVP slips will help you finalize your seat plan and update your seat requirements.

When creating your seat plan, be sure to put together people who have already met before to avoid dull moments for your guests – although, the idea of having them meet new people is also a good thought. If you're not sure about this, discreetly ask them who they would want to sit with and who they'd want to avoid. At least with that, you'll never go wrong.

Entertainment

It is to be assumed that you have already booked your entertainment beforehand, but you may want to check with them if they've got everything covered. At least one week prior to the event, call or visit your entertainment provider and see if there are some things they would still need for the party (or if they will be able to make it, so you could avoid last-minute cancellations and on-the-spot searches for missing equipment).

If you are hiring singers, you may also want to brief them on the type of event you're having so they could also adjust their playlist for you. Provide them with useful information such as the number of your guests, the type of event, and the average age of your participants.

Guest Speakers (if applicable)

Reconfirm with your guest speakers. It is possible that they have overlooked and double-booked your event date, so it would be wise to remind him that they have appointment with you. Do this a week before the event and then the day before the event, to make sure everything is all set.

Check if your speakers also require anything for their speeches (such as presentations, an overhead projector, a computer, or any additional equipment for other kinds of media).

Chapter 6

During and After your Event

During your event, your main concern is to supervise everyone and everything. It will be your responsibility to make sure everything is working well, and that all issues are resolved right then and there.

Right before your event starts, it is only proper to brief your crew as to how you want the event to turn out and their roles in making the event happen. It is a given point that you have already told them what they should wear and what event it would be, so the on-the-day briefing will be more of a reminder of what they should do.

When all things have been set up and the venue is as you've envisioned it, it is time to put on a great show. During the event, move around as much as you can to make sure everything's fine. Check the supply and quality of food before it comes out from the kitchen. See if every amplifier and microphone is working, check on your speakers if they have all they need and see if your guests are fine.

If it is your own party, it is important that you welcome them personally in a warm manner.

It is also important for you to be seen by your guests, so they could alert you if they have any concern. If this is not your party and you are contracted to be the planner, it is important for you to support the person throwing the event. Constantly ask whether your assistance is needed.

After the event and after sending your guests Thank You cards (also checking whether they've enjoyed the party), it is time to evaluate. Evaluating your event would give you an idea of how you should do the next one. It is done to help you pinpoint where the event went wrong, and what are the things that went well for you. The comments and suggestions of your guests will also help you pick different contractors (or convince you to stay with your trusted suppliers for the next event).

Some service providers require payment before they provide you with whatever it is that they offer. Some will only require your down payment, while others will only collect your full payment after the event. The post-event phase should be the time to settle all your liabilities and check your finances. After all your debts have been paid, do you still have enough for the charity you made the event for? Did you make some profit or did you break even?

After your so-called project, you should be able to see some possibilities for the next one after you've drawn some conclusions on how you could improve.

Chapter 7

More Things to Consider

There are a still lot of things you have to remember before, during, and after your event:

1. A checklist is a helpful tool. Create a checklist that you could carry around, unless you're not afraid of overlooking a crucial detail.

2. No event has ever been done flawlessly. Events are always prone to mistakes and miscalculations. Be ready in case your worst fears come to life during the party. But then again, if you're ready, then it's not the worst, right?

3. Team-up with competent people. Cost is not equal to quality. When choosing your suppliers, choose only the best ones that will be able to give you more than what you paid. It's not enough that you've found the cheapest, you should always go for quality.

4. Create the perfect ambiance. If you want a lively party, then create a scene fit for that party's theme.

5. Each part of it counts. From the faintest color of your surroundings, to the overall taste and quality of food, to the music played, and the memories made – each element of your event should be coherent and come together perfectly.

6. Make your guests feel special. They made the effort of coming and supporting your party, so it's just right to thank them and make them feel special. Addressing their issues (or at least helping them out with it) and meeting their demands would be more than enough.

7. Stay calm. No one can really work well in a stressed environment, and if people see that you're panicking, they'd panic too.

   Whatever the party may throw at you, keep your cool and try to resolve things gracefully.

Conclusion

Thank you very much for downloading this book and letting me help you create a magical and successful event.

The next thing you'd have to do is to take out that planner and pen, and start drafting the best party ever! Open your mind to new ideas. Thinking outside the box will make you see things in a different perspective, making you even more creative.

Again, thank you and good luck!

Published by: MCJ Publishing
www.book-o-rama.com